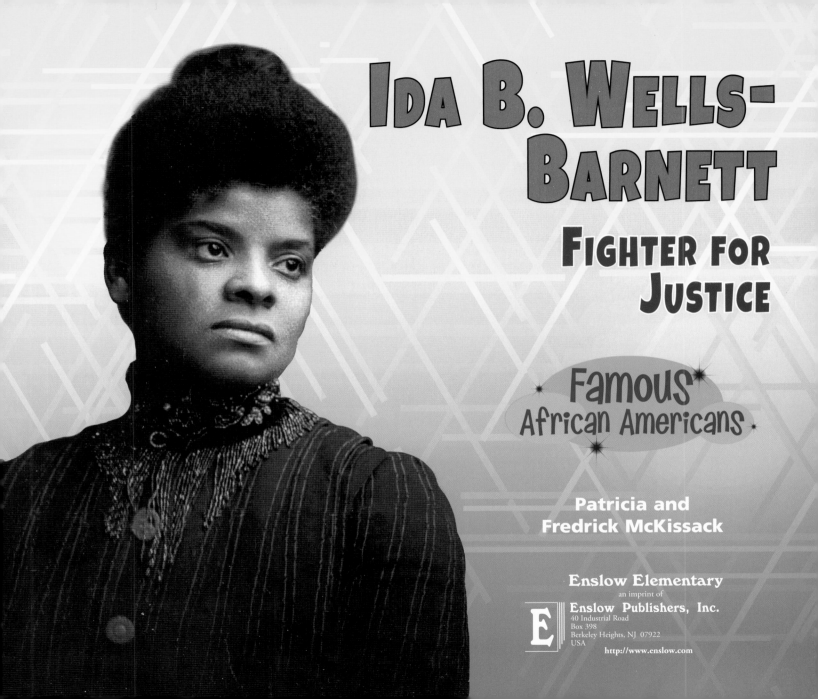

IDA B. WELLS-BARNETT

FIGHTER FOR JUSTICE

Famous African Americans

Patricia and Fredrick McKissack

Enslow Elementary
an imprint of
Enslow Publishers, Inc.
40 Industrial Road
Box 398
Berkeley Heights, NJ 07922
USA

http://www.enslow.com

For Ann and Jerome Hamilton

Enslow Elementary, an imprint of Enslow Publishers, Inc.

Enslow Elementary® is a registered trademark of Enslow Publishers, Inc.

Revised edition of *Ida B. Wells-Barnett: A Voice Against Violence* © 1991

Library of Congress Cataloging-in-Publication Data

McKissack, Pat, 1944-
     McKissack, Pat, 1944-
     Ida B. Wellsbarnett : fighter for justice / Patricia and Fredrick McKissack.
        p. cm. — (Famous African Americans)
     Previously published: Berkeley Heights, NJ : Enslow Publishers, c2001.
     Summary: "A simple biography about Ida B. Wells Barnett for early readers"—Provided by publisher.
     Includes bibliographical references and index.
     ISBN 978-0-7660-4108-0
     1. Wells-Barnett, Ida B., 1862-1931—Juvenile literature. 2. African American women civil rights workers—Biography—Juvenile literature. 3. Civil rights workers—United States—Biography—Juvenile literature. 4. Journalists—United States—Biography—Juvenile literature. 5. African Americans—Social conditions—Juvenile literature. 6. Lynching—United States—History—Juvenile literature. 7. United States—Race relations—Juvenile literature. I. McKissack, Fredrick. II. Title.
     E185.97.W55M37 2013
     323.092—dc23
     [B]
                              2012019033

Future editions:
Paperback ISBN: 978-1-4644-0198-5
ePUB ISBN: 978-1-4645-1111-0
PDF ISBN: 978-1-4646-1111-7

Printed in the United States of America

092012 Lake Book Manufacturing, Inc., Melrose Park, IL

10 9 8 7 6 5 4 3 2 1

To Our Readers: We have done our best to make sure all Internet addresses in this book were active and appropriate when we went to press. However, the author and the publisher have no control over and assume no liability for the material available on those Internet sites or on other Web sites they may link to. Any comments or suggestions can be sent by e-mail to comments@enslow.com or to the address on the back cover.

♻ Enslow Publishers, Inc., is committed to printing our books on recycled paper. The paper in every book contains 10% to 30% post-consumer waste (PCW). The cover board on the outside of each book contains 100% PCW. Our goal is to do our part to help young people and the environment too!

Words in bold type are are explained in Words to Know on page 22.

Photo Credits: Department of Special Collections, University of Chicago Library, pp. 1, 3, 4, 10, 18, 21.

Illustration Credits: Ned O., pp. 7, 8, 10, 13, 14

Cover Photo: Department of Special Collections, University of Chicago Library

Series Consultant:
Russell Adams, PhD
     Emeritus Professor
     Afro-American Studies
     Howard University

CONTENTS

Ida B. Wells loved to write when she was young. When she grew up, she wrote about equal rights and unfair laws.

CHAPTER 1
FEVER!

. . . .

The **Civil War** ended in 1865, and so did **slavery** in America. Jim and Lizzie Wells were freed. So was their three-year-old daughter, Ida. The family lived in Holly Springs, Mississippi. Seven more children were born.

Ida was sent to school. Learning was easy for her. She liked to read, but writing was more fun. She made her parents proud. Besides being smart, Ida Wells grew into a pretty girl with honey-brown skin. She was also loving and kind.

Then came the fever! **Yellow fever** was a killer **disease**. There was no cure at that time. Many good people died in Holly Springs. Jim and Lizzie were among them. So was their baby son.

Ida was just sixteen years old. Their Holly Springs neighbors wanted to take the children to live with them. But Ida kept her family together. They lived in the house her parents left for them. She got a job as a country school teacher to earn money.

The next year, Ida let other family members take the children. Ida moved to Memphis, Tennessee, and got another job teaching there.

Ida got a job teaching children to earn money for her family.

CHAPTER 2
FIRST FIGHT FOR FREEDOM

· ·

After the Civil War, laws were passed that protected the rights of all Americans regardless of color. Blacks had the same rights as whites. They rode in train cars together, sat together in public places, and shared the same public drinking fountains. But by 1878, laws began to change.

Ida taught in a one-room schoolhouse near Memphis. She rode the train into town at the end of each week.

One day Ida bought a train ticket to Memphis. She sat in the front car. The conductor told Ida to move to the car where men who smoked rode. It was called a **smoker car**.

Why? She was black. For many years, it was against the law to make people sit in separate cars because of their color. Ida did not know that this law had changed. She would not move. The conductor took her arm. She bit him. He called for help. Another man came. They picked Ida up and made her move.

Ida fought against the men who tried to make her change seats on the train.

No one helped her. Ida would not sit in the smoker car. Instead she got off the train.

Ida was very angry. She was just twenty-one years old, but she decided to fight for her rights another way. She took the railroad company to court. She found a lawyer to take her case. Months passed. Nothing happened. Ida learned that her lawyer had been paid off by the railroad. She found another lawyer.

Finally, the case went to court. Ida won her case. The judge ordered the railroad company to pay Ida $500. It was her first fight for freedom!

The railroad took the case to another court, and this time, Ida lost.

From 1880 to 1900, states passed more laws that took away black people's rights. Ida would always speak out against unfair laws.

CHAPTER 3
VIOLENCE

. . . .

Ida Wells went to Rust College in Holly Springs, and Fisk University in Nashville, Tennessee.

She still taught school in Memphis. Often Ida spoke out about how poor black schools were. She wrote for a church newspaper, **The Living Way**. She spoke up about rights and fair laws. Soon she was asked to write for other black newspapers, too.

In 1889, Ida became part owner of a Memphis newspaper, **Free Speech**. Once she wrote about black schools in Memphis. She said they were run-down and crowded, and there were not enough books. Ida lost her teaching job after that. But she did not stop speaking out.

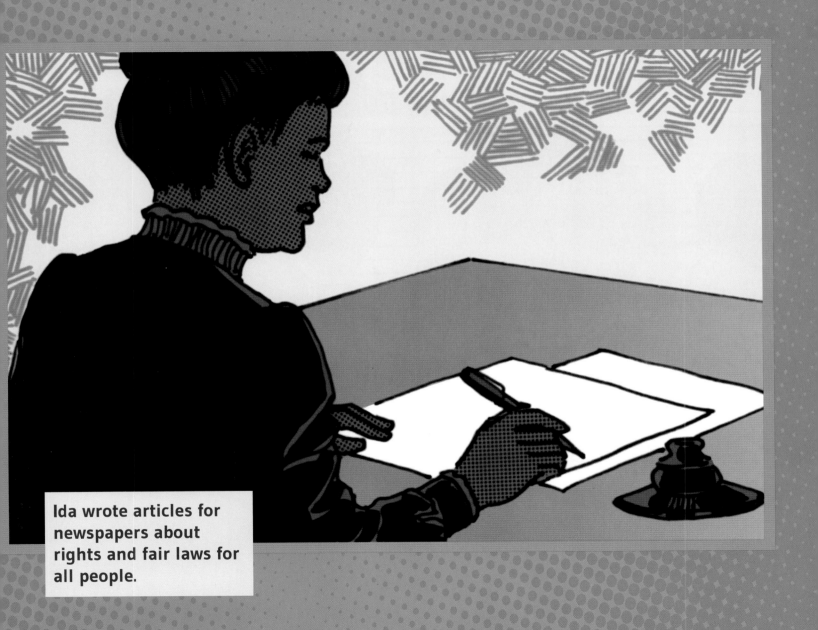

Ida wrote articles for newspapers about rights and fair laws for all people.

Laws were passed that made it hard for black people to vote.

In many southern states, laws were being passed that took away the rights of African Americans. Some laws made it very hard for blacks to vote. When blacks tried to vote they were beaten. Their houses and businesses were burned. Many times they were hanged. Murdering people this way was called **lynching**.

Ida wrote about these terrible beatings, house burnings, and lynchings. She spoke out against the unfair laws that were being passed. Friends told her to be careful. Maybe she should stop. No! She would keep writing the stories.

Then, in 1892, three young black men were shot to death. They had done nothing wrong. Ida wanted people to protest this tragedy. ". . . Say or do something," Ida wrote. Very few people said or did anything.

Finally, a group of angry men burned the office of *Free Speech*. Ida got away just in time.

Running wasn't easy for Ida. She wanted to stay in Memphis and fight against **violence**. Her friends said, go North. Go where it will be safe to speak out!

And so she did. Ida B. Wells went to New York. Her work was not over. It was really just beginning.

CHAPTER 4
THE STRUGGLE AGAINST VIOLENCE

Ida worked for the **New York Age** newspaper in New York. T. Thomas Fortune was the owner. He said Ida "had plenty of nerve." Those who knew Ida agreed with Mr. Fortune's words.

In 1893, Ida decided to move to Chicago. There she began writing for an African-American newspaper owned by Ferdinand L. Barnett. Ida went all over the United States and Europe asking people to join her in her fight. Thousands and thousands of people joined her.

In 1895, Ida wrote a small book named **The Red Record**. It showed that thousands of black men, women, and children had been lynched. Something had to be done to stop the violence against black people.

On June 27, 1895, Ida married Ferdinand L. Barnett. Many people wondered, would Ida give up her work? Not for long. When her first son, Charles, was six months old, Ida Wells-Barnett went back to work. With baby Charles at her side, she spoke all over the country. She even spoke to the **president** of the United States.

In 1898, Ida met with President William McKinley at the White House. She told him that ten thousand black men, women, and children had been lynched since the Civil War.

The president said he was shocked, but he did little to help. There was still violence. The fight against it went on, too. Ida Wells-Barnett made sure of that.

Ida with her son, Charles, in 1896.

CHAPTER 5
No More Lynching!

Ida was not the only person speaking out against lynching. Other women joined her. They formed clubs called the Ida B. Wells Clubs. No more lynching! was their cry.

Women could not vote. Ida worked for women's rights, too. But it wasn't until 1920 that American women were given the right to vote.

She was also interested in children's rights. Ida pushed for better laws that protected children from violence, too.

In 1908, there was a **race riot** in Springfield, Illinois. More killing . . . more burning. White and black Americans met in New York. Ida Wells-Barnett attended. Something had to be done about the lynchings, beatings, and burnings. Out of that meeting came the **National Association for the Advancement of Colored People** (NAACP). The NAACP was formed in 1909 to help work for rights through the courts. The NAACP was also against the **Ku Klux Klan** (KKK), a hate group formed right after the Civil War.

For many years the KKK had not been very strong. But in 1915 the secret group started up again on Stone Mountain in Georgia. KKK members used violence and fear against people of color, Jews, and Catholics.

Ida Wells-Barnett worked all her life to stop the Ku Klux Klan. No more lynching! was her battle cry.

When the spring flowers bloomed in 1931, Ida B. Wells-Barnett got sick. Two days later, she died. Twenty years later, there was only one lynching reported in the United States. Ida's work had made a difference.

Ida spent her life trying to end violence against African Americans.

WORDS TO KNOW

civil war—A war fought within one country. In the United States, the Civil War (1861–1865) was fought between northern and southern states.

disease—An illness or sickness.

Ku Klux Klan (KKK)—A race-hate group started after the Civil War.

The Living Way—A black church newspaper in Memphis, Tennessee, in the 1800s.

lynching—Illegal killing, usually by hanging; a murder done by a mob of people.

Free Speech—The newspaper Ida B. Wells-Barnett co-owned in Memphis, Tennessee.

National Association for the Advancement of Colored People (NAACP)—An organization started to help all Americans gain equal rights and protection under the law. The NAACP is one of the oldest civil rights organizations in the United States.

New York Age—A weekly black newspaper in New York in the late 1800s.

president—The leader of a country or an organization.

race riot—Violence in the streets; violent acts against a race of people.

The Red Record—A book about lynchings, written by Ida B. Wells-Barnett in 1895.

slavery—The buying and selling of human beings.

smoker car—A train car for men who smoked. It was bad manners for men to smoke in front of women.

violence—Acts that hurt or destroy people, places, animals, and other things.

yellow fever—A disease that is carried by mosquitoes. It killed thousands of people in the late 1800s.

Learn More

Books

Frost, Helen. *Let's Meet Ida B. Wells-Barnett*. New York: Chelsea Clubhouse, 2003.

Moore, Heidi. *Ida B. Wells-Barnett*. Chicago: Heinemann, 2004.

Myers, Walter Dean. *Ida B. Wells: Let the Truth Be Told*. New York: Amistad Press, 2008.

Web Sites

African American Perspectives, "The Progress of a People"

<http://lcweb2.loc.gov/ammem/aap/idawells.html>

Ida B. Wells Memorial Foundation

<http://www.idabwells.org>

INDEX